Bethany Joy Revealed

Overcoming Fame, Cult Control, and Rebuilding Her Life

Clever James Publishing

Copyright

Disclaimer

This book is a biographical account based on the life and experiences of Bethany Joy Lenz, as shared through her interviews, public statements, and memoirs. While every effort has been made to accurately represent the events, thoughts, and feelings described by Bethany, some details may reflect her personal recollections and interpretations. Names of certain individuals and organizations, particularly those associated with sensitive or private matters, may have been changed to protect their privacy.

This biography does not intend to provide legal, medical, or psychological advice. It is a personal account, and readers are encouraged to seek professional guidance for any issues relating to trauma, cult involvement, or abuse. The author and

Table of Contents

Introduction

The name Bethany Joy Lenz may instantly evoke images of the beloved character Haley James Scott from One Tree Hill, a role that not only made her a household name but also solidified her position in the pantheon of iconic television stars. Yet, beyond the screen, Lenz's life has been a complex tapestry woven with fame, personal battles, and a deep quest for identity. What many fans may not know is that behind the carefully curated image of success and stability lay a woman grappling with experiences that would shape her in ways few could imagine.

For a decade, Bethany lived a double life, trapped in what she now describes as a high-control religious group—known publicly as The Big House Family—while balancing the pressures of Hollywood. The cult controlled many aspects of her life, from personal relationships to finances, draining millions of dollars from her TV earnings and isolating her from friends and family. And yet, for years, she carried on. She acted, she sang, she smiled for the cameras, all while hiding the pain and confusion she faced behind the scenes.

It wasn't until she became a mother that Bethany found the strength to break free from the manipulative and abusive environment she had been entrenched in. This turning point not only marked a new chapter in her personal life but also fueled her desire to share her story—one that extends beyond the glitz of television fame to something far more universal: the struggle to reclaim one's own life.

In Bethany Joy Revealed: Overcoming Fame, Cult Control, and Rebuilding Her Life, Bethany takes us on an intimate journey of transformation. From her rise as a young star to her hidden decade within a cult, and eventually her courageous path to healing and renewal, this book is not just a biography. It is a testament to resilience, survival, and the power of self-discovery.

This is Bethany's story, in her own words, told with the honesty and grace that fans have come to love. But more than that, it's a story for anyone who has ever felt lost, controlled, or unsure of how to move forward. It's a reminder that no matter how far you may fall, there is always a way to rise again.

As you read Bethany's remarkable tale, you will not only get a deeper glimpse into her life behind the scenes but also an opportunity to reflect on your own journey. Through her trials and triumphs, Bethany shows us that even in the face of the most profound adversity, there is always hope, and there is always a way to rebuild.

Chapter One

Early Life and Beginnings

Bethany Joy Lenz, born on April 2, 1981, in Hollywood, Florida, grew up in a world far removed from the glittering lights of show business that would later become her stage. Raised as an only child in a household that nurtured creativity, her early life was grounded in the values of faith, community, and the quiet pursuit of artistic expression. Both her parents played significant roles in shaping her outlook on life. Her father, Robert Lenz, was a history teacher and therapist, while her mother, Cathie Lenz, worked as a personnel manager and entrepreneur. This eclectic mix of professions created an environment where learning, compassion, and creativity were equally valued.

From a young age, Bethany was immersed in the arts. She had an inherent love for performing that manifested early in her life. By the age of seven, Bethany was already performing in local theater productions, including musicals and plays, where her natural talent for acting and singing began to shine through. However, her early exposure to the church also had a profound influence on her, not just spiritually but also artistically. Growing up in a Christian household, Bethany's faith was a constant in her life, and she spent much of her childhood involved in the church choir, where her love for music deepened. This foundation in music and faith would later play an important role in her personal and professional journey.

By the time Bethany was a teenager, her talent had become undeniable. Her family decided to move to Dallas, Texas, to provide her with more opportunities to pursue acting. Dallas, with its proximity to both stage productions and regional television, became the place where Bethany would take her first major steps toward becoming a professional actress. Her dedication to her craft was clear from the start. While attending acting classes, she also honed her skills as a singer and musician, determined to make her mark in both areas.

At just 13 years old, Bethany's career began to take off when she was cast as Reva Shayne's teenage clone in the long-running soap opera *Guiding Light*. This role was pivotal, not just because it was her first taste of fame, but because it demanded emotional depth and maturity beyond her years. Working in the fast-paced environment of a soap opera, where shooting schedules are relentless, helped Bethany develop a strong work ethic that would define her career moving forward. The character of Reva Shayne had a dedicated fanbase, and stepping into such a prominent role was a challenge for any young actress, but Bethany's performance was lauded for its authenticity and emotional intensity.

This early success brought Bethany into the public eye, but even as her fame grew, she remained deeply connected to her roots. Her faith, which had been nurtured during her early years, remained an anchor for her in the tumultuous world of television acting. However, the intensity of working in Hollywood at such a young age also led Bethany down a path that would change her life in unexpected ways. At 20, while navigating the complexities of her rising fame, Bethany was introduced to a Bible study group that promised emotional support and spiritual growth for young actors like herself. What initially appeared to be a welcoming community soon revealed itself to be far more sinister.

As her career continued to flourish, Bethany found herself increasingly drawn into the influence of a high-control religious group known as The Big House Family. What began as a place of solace and community quickly transformed into a toxic environment that dominated her personal and financial life. The group, which she later revealed as an abusive and manipulative cult, slowly eroded her independence, leading her to make choices that would isolate her from friends, family, and colleagues. This period marked a sharp departure from the hopeful beginnings of her early career.

Despite these personal struggles, Bethany's professional career was thriving. In 2003, she landed the role that would define her public persona—Haley James Scott on the hit television series *One Tree Hill*. For nearly a decade, Bethany played the wholesome, down-to-earth Haley, whose storylines often mirrored aspects of her real life. On-screen, Haley balanced her love for music, her strong moral compass, and her role as a supportive friend and partner. Off-screen, Bethany was grappling with the loss of her own autonomy as she became more deeply enmeshed in the cult.

The parallels between Bethany's personal life and her character's journey on *One Tree Hill* were striking. Both Haley and Bethany faced struggles with identity, independence, and finding a sense of self in environments that demanded conformity. In interviews years later, Bethany reflected on how playing Haley became a form of escapism for her—a way to channel her emotions into her work while struggling privately with the pressures of her real-life situation.

Her deep commitment to her faith, which had always been a source of strength, was twisted by the manipulative teachings of the cult leaders. They convinced her to marry one of the leader's sons, a decision that was dictated by the cult's strict hierarchy rather than her own desires. This marriage, which was devoid of the love and partnership she had longed for, further trapped Bethany in a life she had not chosen for herself.

For over a decade, Bethany remained in the grip of the cult, during which time they took control of nearly every aspect of her life—emotionally, financially, and spiritually. She was persuaded to give up large sums of money, disconnect from her family, and isolate herself from the friends and colleagues who could have helped her. By the time she realized the full extent of the group's manipulation, it seemed impossible to leave. The fear of losing everything—her career, her financial stability, her community—kept her in the group far longer than she had ever intended.

Her breakthrough came with the birth of her daughter in 2011. Becoming a mother gave Bethany the clarity and courage she needed to reassess her life. The responsibility of caring for another human being forced her to confront the toxic control the cult had over her. Slowly, Bethany began to disentangle herself from the group's influence, seeking therapy and reconnecting with the people she had pushed away during her years of isolation. Her decision to leave the cult marked a turning point in her life, both personally and professionally.

Though leaving the group was incredibly difficult, it was also a profound moment of liberation. Bethany later spoke about the emotional turmoil of starting over—leaving her marriage, her community, and the life she had built for over a decade. She returned to acting and music with a renewed sense of purpose, determined to regain control of her narrative and create a life that aligned with her true values.

Her early life and career, which had been marked by such promise and hope, had taken a detour into a world of manipulation and control, but Bethany's resilience and unwavering faith in herself allowed her to break free and start anew. The lessons she learned during this period shaped not only her career choices but also the way she viewed her role as a mother, actress, and artist. Today, Bethany Joy Lenz continues to work in the entertainment industry, but her approach is very different. No longer driven by the need for external validation or the demands of others, she has learned to prioritize her own well-being and the well-being of her daughter.

Chapter Two

The Rise of a Star: *One Tree Hill*

When Bethany Joy Lenz was cast in *One Tree Hill*, she had no idea just how profoundly it would shape her life. The role of Haley James Scott became a defining moment in her career, catapulting her from a relatively unknown actress to one of the most recognizable faces on television during the early 2000s. However, the journey wasn't just about fame and success. Beneath the surface of her rising stardom lay deeper struggles that would only come to light much later, painting a complex portrait of a woman balancing professional success with personal turmoil.

In the early 2000s, *One Tree Hill* was a sensation, drawing in viewers with its mix of teenage drama, romance, and the pursuit of dreams. For Bethany, landing the role of Haley James was both an opportunity and a challenge. At the time, she was best known for her soap opera work, particularly for her role on *Guiding Light*. However, *One Tree Hill* offered her something far different: the chance to play a character that would become beloved by fans worldwide, a role that would span almost a decade. What set Haley apart was her relatability. Unlike many of the glamorous characters often seen in television dramas, Haley was grounded, kind-hearted, and authentic. Bethany infused the character with depth, and her portrayal resonated with audiences who saw themselves in Haley's struggles and triumphs.

From the very first season, it was clear that Haley's character would play a significant role in the show's narrative. Initially introduced as Lucas Scott's best friend, Haley's arc quickly expanded when she entered into a romantic relationship with Nathan Scott, the school's basketball star. The chemistry between Bethany Joy Lenz and James Lafferty, who played Nathan, became a central element of the show's success. The dynamic between Haley and Nathan—often referred to as "Naley" by fans—was more than just a teenage romance. It explored themes of love, commitment, and the challenges of growing up together. For many viewers, the relationship symbolized hope, resilience, and the belief that love can withstand the test of time, making Bethany's role all the more iconic.

However, while Bethany's professional life was soaring, her personal life was far more complicated. During her time on *One Tree Hill*, she was living a double life. Behind the scenes, she was deeply involved with a group that she later revealed to be a cult. The cult, which initially appeared to be a harmless Bible study group, slowly ensnared her into a world of control, manipulation, and isolation. For a period of nearly ten years, Bethany was a part of what she describes as an "abusive, high-demand group." This experience affected every aspect of her life, including her relationships with her *One Tree Hill* co-stars. It was an isolating experience, as the cult encouraged her to distance herself from those who were not part of the group, even including her castmates.

At the time, Bethany did her best to keep up appearances. To the public and even to her colleagues on set, she was a talented actress navigating the challenges of fame. But behind closed doors, she was dealing with pressures that none of them fully understood. It wasn't until years later, after leaving the cult, that Bethany began to open up about the ordeal. In her own words, she was trapped in a situation where she didn't even realize the extent of the control the group had over her until it was too late. The cult took a significant toll on her mental and emotional well-being, leaving her to question her identity and purpose, even as her public persona was celebrated.

Despite these challenges, Bethany remained committed to her work on *One Tree Hill*, using her role as a form of escape from the reality she was living off-screen. The character of Haley, with her steadfast values and loving nature, became a way for Bethany to channel her emotions and find stability in a world that was otherwise chaotic. In a sense, playing Haley was a lifeline, allowing Bethany to focus on something positive while navigating the complexities of her personal life. Her dedication to the role earned her not only critical acclaim but also a fiercely loyal fan base. Viewers admired Haley's journey from a small-town tutor to a wife, mother, and professional musician, and Bethany's authentic portrayal made Haley's story all the more believable.

Bethany's talents weren't limited to acting alone. Throughout the series, her musical abilities were also highlighted. Haley's character often showcased her singing, a reflection of Bethany's real-life passion for music. In fact, her involvement in music was more than just a plot point in the show. Bethany had been working on her music career long before *One Tree Hill* and continued to pursue it alongside her acting. During her time on the show, she even went on a music tour with fellow cast members, performing songs from the show's soundtracks. The music was another outlet for Bethany to express herself, and fans were quick to embrace her dual talents as both an actress and a singer.

As the show progressed, Bethany took on even more responsibilities. In the sixth season, she made her directorial debut, an experience that was both challenging and rewarding. Directing gave her a new perspective on storytelling and allowed her to have greater creative input in the show she had come to love. It also demonstrated her versatility and ambition as a creative professional, proving that she was more than just a talented actress—she was a storyteller in every sense of the word.

The success of *One Tree Hill* extended far beyond its original run. The show developed a cult following, with fans continuing to watch and rewatch episodes years after it went off the air. For Bethany, the legacy of *One Tree Hill* is something she cherishes, though she has also had to reconcile her feelings about the period in her life when the show was at its peak. It was during these years that she was also dealing with the dark reality of her involvement in the cult. Looking back, Bethany has described how difficult it was to maintain the illusion of normalcy while grappling with such deep personal struggles. Yet, through it all, she continued to deliver powerful performances that resonated with viewers.

In recent years, Bethany has become more open about her experiences, using her platform to discuss the dangers of high-control groups and the importance of personal freedom. Her decision to share her story was not an easy one, but she felt a responsibility to speak out, not just for herself, but for others who might be in similar situations. Her revelations have been met with both support and shock, as many fans had no idea what she had been enduring during her time on *One Tree Hill*.

As *One Tree Hill* came to an end after nine seasons, Bethany found herself at a crossroads. She had spent nearly a decade portraying a character who had become an integral part of her identity, both on-screen and off. The end of the show marked the beginning of a new chapter in her life—one where she would finally confront the challenges that had been brewing beneath the surface for so long. She left the cult, began the difficult process of rebuilding her life, and sought therapy to address the trauma she had experienced. The journey was far from easy, but Bethany approached it with the same resilience and determination that she had shown throughout her career.

Today, Bethany Joy Lenz stands as a symbol of strength and survival. Her experiences on *One Tree Hill* are forever intertwined with the personal battles she faced during that time, but they also represent a period of growth and self-discovery. She has since gone on to pursue new creative projects, including her work in music and film, as well as co-hosting the *Drama Queens* podcast with her former co-stars Sophia Bush and Hilarie Burton. Through it all, she remains grateful for the opportunities she's had, the lessons she's learned, and the chance to use her story to inspire others.

Chapter Three

Directorial Debut and Creative Ventures

Bethany Joy Lenz has long been admired for her multifaceted talents—most notably her acting on the hit series *One Tree Hill*, where she captivated audiences as Haley James Scott. Yet, beyond her remarkable performances on screen, Bethany harbored a creative vision that extended behind the camera, seeking to leave her imprint on the world of directing and producing. Her journey to realizing this ambition was not just a career milestone but also a defining moment in her personal evolution, as she sought greater artistic control and a broader platform to express her creativity.

Bethany's directorial debut came during the sixth season of *One Tree Hill*, a moment that marked both personal and professional growth for the actress. She had first expressed her interest in directing early in the show's run, approaching producer Greg Prange in 2007 with her desire to step behind the camera. However, at the time, her request wasn't immediately granted. It took two years of persistence, observation, and learning for her to finally be given the opportunity to direct an episode of the show that had defined much of her career. During this period, Bethany was dedicated to mastering the craft. She shadowed directors, attended location scouts, and familiarized herself with the technicalities of the job, preparing diligently for her role as a director. Her commitment paid off in 2009 when she directed her first episode of *One Tree Hill*, marking a significant milestone in her career.

Bethany's foray into directing was a deeply personal one. Directing allowed her to channel her artistic expression in a new way, providing a sense of agency over how the story was told, and it aligned with her broader quest for personal empowerment. During her time on *One Tree Hill*, Bethany's life was marked by an internal struggle that wasn't visible to the outside world. While her career soared, she was grappling with the pressures of fame and the constraints of her personal life. Behind the scenes, she was living a double life, caught up in a controlling religious group—a cult—that manipulated and restricted her freedom. Her involvement with the cult, known as The Big House Family, had started innocently enough, as a Bible study group for creatives in Hollywood, but it soon grew into something far more insidious.

For Bethany, directing was not only a professional triumph but also a way to reclaim her sense of self. The creative control that directing offered contrasted sharply with the oppressive environment she faced in her personal life. In the cult, her independence was stifled, and she was subjected to manipulation, financial exploitation, and emotional control. The experience drained her of millions of dollars from her television income, left her in an abusive marriage to the cult leader's son, and alienated her from her closest friends and family. But through the creative process of directing, she found a sense of liberation. Each step behind the camera was a quiet act of defiance against the forces in her personal life that sought to confine her.

Bethany's time as a director on *One Tree Hill* also reflected her broader ambitions as an artist. She wasn't content to be seen merely as an actress delivering lines written by someone else. She wanted to be a storyteller, a creator who could shape the narratives that audiences connected with on an emotional level. This desire extended into other aspects of her creative ventures, particularly her music. Throughout her career, music had been a form of personal expression for Bethany. She was not only a talented singer but also a songwriter and musician. Her passion for music, much like her passion for directing, was rooted in a deep need to connect with audiences on a more profound level.

During her time on *One Tree Hill*, Bethany continued to release music, much of which reflected her personal struggles and triumphs. Her songs were often introspective, touching on themes of love, loss, and personal growth. Her collaboration with her co-stars, such as Tyler Hilton, on songs like "When the Stars Go Blue" helped to solidify her reputation as not only an actress but also a serious musician. She formed the band Everly with her lifelong friend Amber Sweeney, further expanding her musical horizons. The band's acoustic-driven sound, filled with rich harmonies and heartfelt lyrics, resonated with fans who admired Bethany's ability to convey emotion through both her acting and her music.

Music, much like directing, became a refuge for Bethany. It was a way for her to process the challenges she was facing in her personal life while also remaining true to her artistic roots. For years, she used her music as a form of escapism, a place where she could express the parts of herself that the cult had tried to suppress. The songs she wrote were not only about heartbreak and hope but also about resilience and the determination to overcome obstacles, themes that reflected her real-life struggles.

As she transitioned from directing episodes of *One Tree Hill* to focusing on her music, Bethany faced another significant turning point in her life. The show wrapped after nine seasons, leaving Bethany at a crossroads. While her character Haley James Scott had become an iconic figure in television, Bethany was eager to explore new creative opportunities that would allow her to grow as an artist. However, it was also during this time that she began to confront the full extent of the control the cult had over her life. With the show ending and her personal life in turmoil, Bethany started to take steps toward breaking free from the group.

Her departure from the cult was not an easy process. It required immense courage to leave behind the life she had built within the group, including her marriage and friendships. Yet, directing had given her a taste of what it felt like to be in control of her own narrative, and she was determined to reclaim that power in her personal life. Therapy played a crucial role in her escape, helping her to set boundaries and confront the emotional trauma she had endured. As Bethany began to distance herself from the cult, she also started to rebuild her career on her own terms, seeking out roles and projects that aligned with her values and artistic vision.

In the years following *One Tree Hill*, Bethany continued to explore her creative interests. She took on guest roles in television shows like *Dexter* and *Agents of S.H.I.E.L.D.*, demonstrating her versatility as an actress. She also starred in independent films, including *Grace*, directed by her close friend Kristin Fairweather. These projects allowed Bethany to step out of the shadow of her *One Tree Hill* persona and showcase her range as an artist.

Her creative ventures weren't limited to acting and music. In recent years, Bethany has embraced new platforms to connect with her audience. She co-hosts the popular podcast *Drama Queens* with her former *One Tree Hill* co-stars Sophia Bush and Hilarie Burton, where they reflect on their experiences filming the show and share behind-the-scenes stories. The podcast has been a hit with fans, offering a nostalgic look at the series while also allowing Bethany to engage with a new generation of listeners.

Through it all, Bethany's journey as a director and creative artist has been a testament to her resilience and determination. While she faced immense challenges in her personal life, including the emotional and financial toll of her involvement in the cult, she never lost sight of her artistic ambitions. Directing allowed her to take back control of her narrative, both on and off the screen. It gave her the confidence to confront the darker aspects of her life and ultimately emerge stronger on the other side.

Chapter Four

Life Behind the Scenes: Struggles with the Cult

Bethany Joy Lenz, known for her iconic role as Haley James Scott on *One Tree Hill*, became a household name during the early 2000s. Her life on-screen, however, was far different from the tumultuous and painful reality she lived off-camera. As she rose to fame, Bethany found herself entangled in what she would later reveal as a controlling, abusive cult. This chapter of her life is both haunting and inspiring, showcasing her struggle to regain control of her identity and future.

At the height of her fame, Bethany was drawn to a religious group that she initially believed would offer her the community and spiritual guidance she craved. She had just joined *One Tree Hill*, a show that became a massive success and catapulted her into the limelight. However, fame can be a double-edged sword. While her career soared, Bethany privately struggled with loneliness and uncertainty about the world around her. She longed for a deeper connection, for meaning beyond the glamour and superficiality of Hollywood. This vulnerability made her the perfect target for a manipulative group that preyed on individuals seeking belonging and purpose.

At first, the group appeared innocent enough. It was described to her as a Bible study circle, offering camaraderie with other creatives and actors in Los Angeles. But what began as a spiritual sanctuary quickly devolved into something more sinister. The group, known as the Big House Family, operated under the guise of Christianity, luring people in with promises of spiritual enlightenment and community. Bethany, raised in a Christian household, was drawn to the prospect of deepening her faith and building meaningful connections. She attended meetings, made friends, and slowly became more involved in the group's activities.

Over time, however, the group's leaders exerted more control over her life. They demanded unquestioning obedience, cut her off from her family, and instructed her to isolate herself from people they deemed "dangerous" or "ungodly." As Bethany's involvement deepened, her relationships outside the group began to deteriorate. She stopped communicating with friends, distanced herself from her family, and began turning down lucrative film roles. Despite her success on *One Tree Hill*, the group convinced her that fame was sinful, that she needed to focus on a higher calling — serving their cause. They began controlling her finances, and, as Bethany later revealed, she was coerced into giving away millions of her earnings to the group, believing it was part of her spiritual duty.

During this time, Bethany married one of the sons of the group's leader, a decision she admits was not made out of love, but out of pressure and manipulation. The marriage became another tool the group used to control her, imposing strict rules on her relationship and demanding that she adhere to their version of marriage, which was devoid of emotional intimacy and genuine connection. The physical and emotional toll of this arrangement was devastating. Bethany revealed in later interviews that she suffered from PTSD due to the psychological manipulation she endured in the marriage. Her life within the group was stifling, and while her on-screen character, Haley, was experiencing the highs and lows of marriage and motherhood, Bethany's real-life relationship was cold and controlled, leaving her emotionally drained.

Despite the deep psychological hold the group had over her, Bethany began to sense that something was terribly wrong. As the years passed, she felt increasingly conflicted between her faith, her career, and the cult's demands. She started to see the cracks in their teachings, realizing that the group was less about spirituality and more about control. She felt torn between her desire to be a good Christian and her growing awareness that the cult's practices were far from what she believed Christianity should be. Yet, the fear of losing everything—her friends, her marriage, her community—kept her trapped. Leaving the group would mean not only losing her sense of belonging but also facing the truth that she had been manipulated for years.

It wasn't until she became a mother that Bethany found the strength to break free. The birth of her daughter was a turning point. For the first time, she began to question the cult's teachings on a deeper level, recognizing that the environment she was in was not one she wanted her child to grow up in. Bethany realized that she needed to protect her daughter, even if it meant losing everything she had built over the years. Her escape from the cult was not immediate or easy. It took time, therapy, and the support of unlikely allies, including a fan of *One Tree Hill* who helped her realize that she deserved a better life outside the cult's control.

When Bethany finally broke free, she was left with the monumental task of rebuilding her life. She had lost millions of dollars, her marriage had crumbled, and she had to come to terms with the psychological damage the group had inflicted on her. The road to recovery was long and painful. Therapy became a vital part of her healing process, helping her set boundaries and reclaim her independence. It was during these therapy sessions that she began to confront the trauma she had endured, including the emotional and psychological abuse she suffered at the hands of the cult's leaders. This period of her life was marked by deep introspection and self-discovery, as she worked to untangle the lies she had been fed for years.

Despite the trauma, Bethany's faith remained intact, though it took on a different form. She began to reexamine her relationship with God, separating the teachings of the cult from the spirituality she still cherished. Bethany has been candid in interviews about how difficult it was to rebuild her faith after such a betrayal, but she never lost hope. Her journey toward spiritual healing is ongoing, but she has made it clear that she no longer allows others to define her relationship with her faith. She has reclaimed her spirituality on her terms, without the interference of manipulative figures.

Bethany's decision to speak out about her experience in the cult was not an easy one. For years, she kept her involvement hidden, even from her closest friends and co-stars. It wasn't until she joined her former *One Tree Hill* co-stars, Sophia Bush and Hilarie Burton, on the *Drama Queens* podcast that she began to share the details of her time in the group. Her openness has been met with both admiration and support, as fans and fellow survivors have reached out to her, expressing gratitude for her bravery in sharing her story. By speaking out, Bethany has helped shed light on the dangers of high-control groups and cults, offering hope to those who may find themselves in similar situations.

In 2024, Bethany released her memoir *Dinner for Vampires*, a detailed account of her life in the cult, how she escaped, and the process of rebuilding her life. The memoir has been a cathartic experience for her, allowing her to take control of her narrative and share her story in her own words. In interviews, Bethany has emphasized that the book is not just about the pain she endured, but also about the strength she found in the aftermath. She hopes that her story will serve as a reminder that no matter how dark the circumstances, there is always a way out.

Bethany Joy Lenz's journey from fame to cult control and back to freedom is a testament to her resilience. Her ability to overcome the manipulation and abuse she faced, while maintaining her faith and rebuilding her life, speaks to her inner strength and determination. Today, Bethany continues to act, sing, and pursue creative projects, but her focus has shifted. She is now more dedicated than ever to living authentically, free from the control of others. Through her story, Bethany has not only reclaimed her own life but has also inspired countless others to do the same. Her story is one of survival, redemption, and the power of reclaiming your voice after years of being silenced.

Chapter Five

Breaking Free: The Journey to Self-Rediscovery

Bethany Joy Lenz's journey of self-rediscovery is one of the most compelling narratives to emerge from the entertainment industry in recent years. Known for her successful portrayal of Haley James Scott on *One Tree Hill*, Lenz became a household name in the early 2000s. But behind the scenes, her life was far from glamorous. Over the span of a decade, she found herself entangled in a high-control religious group that she later identified as a cult. This chapter of her life marked a period of profound personal struggle, eventually leading to a courageous and transformative escape.

Lenz's involvement in the cult, known as The Big House Family, began innocently enough. At the age of 20, she was introduced to what seemed like a supportive community of like-minded individuals who shared her faith. Like many others who find themselves in controlling environments, Lenz was searching for a sense of belonging. Her career in Hollywood, despite its apparent success, left her feeling isolated, and she was drawn to the emotional intimacy and connection that the group seemed to offer. The group presented itself as a Bible study gathering, and at first, nothing about it raised any red flags. However, over time, the group's grip on Lenz grew stronger, turning her life into a complex web of manipulation and control.

At the height of her success on *One Tree Hill*, Lenz was living a double life. While fans saw her as a confident, grounded actress, the reality was that she was growing increasingly isolated from her friends, family, and even her co-stars. The leaders of the group encouraged her to cut off contact with people outside the cult, insisting that only they could guide her toward spiritual enlightenment. The emotional and psychological toll of this isolation was immense, leaving Lenz vulnerable to the cult's influence. What's more, the group exploited her financially, draining millions from her acting income over the years.

Despite these challenges, Lenz remained committed to her work on *One Tree Hill*, using her role as Haley James Scott as a form of escapism. The character of Haley became a refuge for her, a place where she could temporarily disconnect from the turmoil of her personal life. On screen, Haley was a beacon of strength and resilience, qualities that Lenz desperately needed in her own life. However, the pressure of maintaining this facade took a heavy toll, and she began to feel the weight of her double life more acutely as the years went on.

One of the most pivotal moments in Lenz's journey came when she became a mother. The birth of her daughter was a transformative experience that shifted her perspective on her life and her involvement in the cult. Suddenly, the stakes were higher. It was no longer just her own well-being at risk, but that of her child. Lenz has spoken candidly about how motherhood gave her the courage to question the teachings and control of the cult, eventually leading her to recognize the toxic environment she had been entrenched in for so long.

The process of breaking free, however, was not instantaneous. Lenz's departure from the cult required immense inner strength and support. It was through the help of a *One Tree Hill* superfan, who had sensed something was wrong, that she began to extricate herself from the group's control. This fan, who had followed Lenz's career closely and had become aware of her struggles, reached out in a way that resonated with Lenz. Their support, coupled with the realization that she needed to protect her daughter from the harmful influence of the cult, motivated her to take the bold step of leaving.

But leaving the cult was only the beginning of Lenz's journey toward self-rediscovery. The emotional scars of her experience were deep, and it took years of therapy and self-reflection to heal from the trauma she had endured. In interviews, Lenz has opened up about how therapy helped her understand the psychological manipulation she had been subjected to and how it affected her sense of identity. The cult had systematically eroded her confidence and autonomy, leaving her with feelings of guilt and shame that she had to work through in order to rebuild her life.

One of the most challenging aspects of Lenz's recovery was coming to terms with the financial and personal losses she had suffered during her time in the cult. The group had not only drained her financially but also caused her to miss out on several major career opportunities. Lenz has shared that she turned down significant roles in film and television because the cult discouraged her from pursuing them, claiming that her involvement in Hollywood was at odds with her spiritual journey. In retrospect, these missed opportunities were painful reminders of the years she had spent under the group's control, but they also fueled her determination to rebuild her career on her own terms.

As Lenz began to regain her independence, she also started to reconnect with her creative passions. Music had always been a significant part of her life, and during her recovery, she found solace in songwriting and performing. Her music became a way for her to process the emotions she had suppressed for so long, allowing her to channel her pain into something healing and beautiful. This period of creative rebirth was essential to her recovery, helping her reclaim her voice both literally and figuratively.

In addition to music, Lenz found new opportunities in acting, taking on roles that aligned with her values and allowed her to explore different facets of her talent. She appeared in various television shows, including *Dexter* and *Agents of S.H.I.E.L.D.*, and made a name for herself in Hallmark movies. These projects, while different from her early work, gave her the space to reinvent herself and establish a new chapter in her career.

Perhaps one of the most significant steps in Lenz's journey of self-rediscovery has been her decision to share her story publicly. For years, she remained silent about her experiences in the cult, unsure of how to untangle the complicated emotions and memories associated with that time. However, as she continued to heal, she recognized the importance of speaking out, not just for herself but for others who might be trapped in similar situations. In recent years, Lenz has used her platform to raise awareness about the dangers of cults and the importance of mental health. Through interviews and her podcast *Drama Queens*, which she co-hosts with her *One Tree Hill* co-stars Sophia Bush and Hilarie Burton, Lenz has been candid about her journey, offering support and solidarity to others who may be struggling.

The release of her memoir, *Dinner for Vampires*, marks a significant milestone in Lenz's recovery. The book, which details her experiences in the cult and her eventual escape, is a testament to her resilience and courage. Writing the memoir was no easy feat, as it required her to confront painful memories and emotions that she had buried for years. However, Lenz has expressed that sharing her story was a necessary step in her healing process, one that allowed her to reclaim her narrative and offer hope to others who have faced similar struggles.

Chapter Six

Rebuilding a Career Post-*One Tree Hill*

After *One Tree Hill* came to an end in 2012, Bethany Joy Lenz found herself standing at a crossroads. For nearly a decade, she had portrayed Haley James Scott, a character beloved by fans for her intelligence, compassion, and resilience. Yet, the conclusion of the show signified more than just the end of a long-running series; it was a turning point in her personal and professional life. The years that followed would be marked by moments of introspection, career challenges, and significant personal transformations, leading her to emerge stronger and more self-aware.

Bethany's post-*One Tree Hill* career began with a focus on diversification. Having spent years playing a character tied to a particular niche, she sought roles that would challenge her acting range and take her beyond the shadow of Haley James Scott. In 2013, she landed a recurring role on *Dexter*, playing Cassie, a woman searching for a quieter life after a successful career in finance. While this role allowed Lenz to explore new facets of her talent, it was still a far cry from the central roles she was accustomed to. Nevertheless, she approached it with her signature dedication, immersing herself fully in the character. It was during this period that Lenz started to realize that her career could not merely be a continuation of her past successes; it required a complete reimagining.

The shift was not without its challenges. In 2015, Lenz was cast in *The Catch*, a Shonda Rhimes-produced drama for ABC. Initially, it seemed like the role of Zoe would be a significant opportunity, but Lenz was replaced before the show aired. The disappointment was palpable, as Lenz had been excited about working with Rhimes, a powerhouse in television. However, rather than seeing this setback as a failure, Lenz embraced it as part of the unpredictable nature of the industry. In a statement to her fans, she was transparent about her feelings, but also expressed encouragement, urging them to still support the show despite her departure.

One of the most significant moments of transformation for Lenz during this period was her decision to speak out about her involvement in a religious cult, known as The Big House Family. For nearly a decade, while simultaneously working on *One Tree Hill*, Lenz had been under the influence of a group that drained her financially, emotionally, and spiritually. She described the experience as one that left her living a "double life," where she appeared confident and successful on the surface, but internally struggled with manipulation and control. The cult leaders had even pressured her into marriage with one of their sons, a relationship that left her feeling trapped and deeply unhappy.

In retrospect, leaving the cult became a key factor in Bethany's process of rebuilding both her personal and professional life. The decision to break free required immense courage, particularly because it meant upending the life she had known for so long. The financial toll was severe—she had lost millions during her time in the group—but the emotional scars were even deeper. Lenz would later reflect on how the experience affected her self-worth and decision-making, often leading her to question her own instincts and desires. However, as she began to disentangle herself from the group's influence, she also started a journey of profound personal healing.

Therapy played a crucial role in this healing process. After leaving the group, Lenz sought professional help to address the emotional trauma she had endured. It was through therapy that she began to understand the depth of the manipulation she had experienced and started to rebuild her sense of self. This period of introspection also led to a renewed focus on her career. She was no longer interested in chasing roles simply for visibility or financial gain; instead, she sought projects that aligned with her evolving values and desire for creative fulfillment.

By 2016, Lenz had re-emerged with a new sense of purpose. She appeared in *American Gothic* and *Agents of S.H.I.E.L.D.*, and while these roles were not as high-profile as her work on *One Tree Hill*, they marked a return to form for Lenz, as she demonstrated her versatility as an actress. She had also been working on independent projects, including short films, which allowed her to take more control over her creative output. At the same time, music continued to play an important role in her life. Lenz had always been a gifted singer-songwriter, and she used this period to further explore her musical interests, releasing songs independently and performing live whenever possible.

Perhaps one of the most significant moments of Lenz's career rebirth came with the launch of the *Drama Queens* podcast in 2021. Reuniting with her *One Tree Hill* co-stars Sophia Bush and Hilarie Burton, the podcast quickly became a hit among fans of the show, offering a behind-the-scenes look at the making of the series. However, for Lenz, *Drama Queens* represented more than just a nostalgic return to the past. It provided a platform for her to reconnect with her fans on her own terms, sharing her experiences in a way that was authentic and empowering. The podcast also allowed her to reflect on the complexities of fame and her personal journey, something that resonated deeply with her audience.

At this point in her career, Lenz had evolved into a multi-faceted artist. Her experiences in

Hollywood and beyond had given her a unique perspective on the entertainment industry, one that she was eager to share with others. In interviews, she often spoke about the importance of mental health and self-care, particularly in an industry that can be unforgiving. She had also become more outspoken about the pressures of being a woman in Hollywood, discussing everything from body image to the challenges of balancing work and personal life. This candidness endeared her even more to her fans, who appreciated her honesty and vulnerability.

As she continued to rebuild her career, Lenz also began to explore new creative avenues. She expressed a desire to return to directing and producing, having first dipped her toes into the world of directing during her time on *One Tree Hill*. Now, with a wealth of personal and professional experiences to draw from, she was eager to take on projects that allowed her to be more involved behind the camera. This marked a significant shift in her career trajectory, as she was no longer just an actress but a storyteller in every sense of the word.

In 2024, Lenz announced the release of her memoir, *Dinner for Vampires*, a book that detailed her experience with the cult and the process of reclaiming her life. The memoir was deeply personal, and in many ways, it was a culmination of the work she had done to rebuild her identity post-*One Tree Hill*. Writing the book was cathartic for Lenz, allowing her to confront her past head-on and share her story with the world. It also solidified her role as not just an actress, but a voice for those who had experienced similar forms of control and manipulation. Through her book, Lenz hoped to provide hope and encouragement to others who might be struggling to find their own way out of difficult situations.

Chapter Seven

Memoir and Public Revelations

Bethany Joy Lenz, known for her breakout role as Haley James Scott on *One Tree Hill*, has lived a life that fans have long admired on screen. However, the actress's personal journey has been far more complex, filled with challenges and transformations that few could have anticipated. Her decision to write her memoir, *Dinner for Vampires*, reveals the depth of her untold story—a tale of overcoming the pressures of fame, breaking free from the control of a religious cult, and rebuilding her life on her own terms.

For over a decade, Lenz kept much of her personal turmoil hidden from the public. Her fans, especially those who grew up watching her on *One Tree Hill*, knew her as the talented, sweet, and dedicated actress who portrayed Haley with remarkable sincerity. But behind the scenes, she was leading a "double life" that deeply impacted her mental, emotional, and financial well-being. This was no ordinary story of celebrity challenges with fame; Bethany found herself caught in the grip of a controlling religious cult during some of her most successful years as an actress. It was a reality she could barely reconcile with her public persona—a talented actress thriving in Hollywood.

Her introduction to what she later described as a "high-control group" came at a vulnerable time in her life. Lenz was young, having just moved to Los Angeles to pursue her acting career, and like many who seek community and belonging in uncertain moments, she found solace in what initially seemed like a supportive religious group. The Big House Family, as it was known, appeared to offer the kind of spiritual connection and emotional intimacy that Lenz craved. At first, it was merely a Bible study group, filled with people who shared her faith and aspirations. However, over time, the group's grip on her life tightened in ways she hadn't anticipated.

Lenz has openly discussed the subtle ways the group exerted control over her. It began with isolating her from her family and friends, under the guise of protecting her spiritual growth. Soon, she found herself questioning those closest to her, believing that they didn't have her best interests at heart. Her castmates on *One Tree Hill* noticed the shift in her behavior, with some sensing that something was wrong, but Lenz wasn't ready to confront it. At the time, she didn't believe she was involved in a cult—she thought she had simply found a group of people who shared her values. But as the manipulation deepened, the group's true nature became clear.

The cult's leader, a domineering pastor, played a significant role in shaping Lenz's personal life, even convincing her to marry his son. The marriage was far from what Lenz had envisioned for herself. She described it as a cold, transactional relationship devoid of the intimacy and emotional connection she so desperately wanted. The group's teachings had warped her understanding of relationships, leading her to believe that her role as a wife was to fulfill her husband's needs, no matter how emotionally detached or unfulfilling the marriage felt. The control extended beyond her personal life and into her professional career. The group discouraged her from pursuing certain acting opportunities and took significant sums of money from her earnings, leaving her in a precarious financial situation despite her success on *One Tree Hill*.

For years, Lenz endured this environment, believing that she was doing the right thing. She had built her entire life around the group, and leaving it meant unraveling everything she knew—her marriage, her friendships, and even her career. But the turning point came when she became a mother. The birth of her daughter gave her a new sense of responsibility and clarity. It was no longer just about her; she had a child to protect and raise in a healthy, loving environment. It was then that Lenz began to see the cult for what it truly was—a manipulative and abusive system that had drained her emotionally, spiritually, and financially.

The decision to leave the group was not easy, nor was it immediate. It took years of therapy and self-reflection for Lenz to fully extricate herself from the cult's influence. Her memoir details the painstaking process of rebuilding her life after leaving the group. She describes how difficult it was to break away from the people she had considered her community, and the fear of starting over with little financial security after the group had taken so much of her earnings. But despite these challenges, Lenz found strength in her newfound independence. Therapy played a crucial role in helping her set boundaries, heal from the emotional trauma of her past, and rebuild her self-esteem.

As she worked to reclaim her life, Lenz also found solace in her work. Acting became more than just a job—it was a form of escapism and a way for her to reconnect with herself. Her role on *One Tree Hill*, particularly her on-screen relationship with James Lafferty's character, Nathan, became a source of comfort. While she didn't develop romantic feelings for Lafferty in real life, their close bond on set provided a safe space for Lenz to process her emotions during some of her darkest times. After the series ended, she continued to take on new roles in both film and television, slowly rebuilding her career and establishing herself as more than just Haley James Scott.

In the years following her departure from the cult, Lenz has been open about the importance of self-care and mental health. She has spoken about the long-lasting effects of her experiences, particularly how they impacted her future relationships and her ability to trust others. One of the most challenging aspects of her recovery was learning to trust herself again. After years of manipulation, she had to relearn how to make decisions based on her own needs and desires, rather than what she had been told was right by others.

Lenz's memoir is more than just a recounting of her time in a cult—it is a story of survival and transformation. It is about how she found the courage to leave an abusive environment, rebuild her life, and find happiness on her own terms. Writing the memoir was, in many ways, a therapeutic process for Lenz. She has described how difficult it was to untangle the web of manipulation and abuse she endured, but ultimately, it was a story she knew she had to share. By opening up about her experiences, she hopes to provide comfort and inspiration to others who may find themselves in similar situations. She has expressed a deep desire to use her platform to raise awareness about the dangers of high-control groups and to encourage others to speak out against abuse in all its forms.

The release of *Dinner for Vampires* has also allowed Lenz to reconnect with her fans in new and meaningful ways. Her honesty and vulnerability have resonated with many, particularly those who grew up watching her on *One Tree Hill* and admired her for the strength she portrayed on screen. Lenz's story serves as a reminder that even those who seem to have it all can face incredible challenges behind closed doors. Her journey is a testament to the power of resilience, and the importance of finding one's own voice, even in the most difficult circumstances.

Chapter Eight

Legacy and Future Projects

Bethany Joy Lenz, a name that resonates deeply with fans of the iconic television show *One Tree Hill*, has crafted an indelible mark in Hollywood through her multifaceted career. But her journey is far more than just a tale of fame and success on screen. As her story continues to unfold, it becomes evident that her legacy is built not only on her artistic talents but also on her remarkable resilience. In recent years, she has revealed deeply personal experiences, including her time in a high-demand cult, her process of healing, and her reemergence as a force in the entertainment industry. This chapter reflects on Bethany's legacy and what her future holds, showing how her life is a beacon of courage, reinvention, and authenticity.

Bethany's early fame was rooted in her role as Haley James Scott on *One Tree Hill*, a character beloved for her intelligence, warmth, and vulnerability. The show itself became a cultural touchstone for many, running for nine seasons and solidifying Lenz's place in the hearts of viewers worldwide. But behind the scenes, Bethany's life was far more complex. As she recently revealed in interviews and through her memoir *Dinner for Vampires*, she spent ten years involved in a religious cult known as The Big House Family. During this time, while she maintained her acting career and public persona, she was privately enduring emotional and financial exploitation. This dichotomy of leading a public life of success while secretly grappling with immense personal struggles has made her story one of profound complexity.

Her decision to speak out about her experience with the cult is a significant aspect of her legacy. For years, Bethany remained silent, unsure of how to reconcile her past with her present. She had been manipulated into a life of control, isolated from friends and family, and subjected to mental and emotional abuse. The cult drained her finances, coerced her into a loveless marriage, and stripped away her autonomy. Yet, when she became a mother, a shift occurred. Her daughter gave her the strength to reevaluate her circumstances and ultimately escape from the toxic environment that had entangled her. This act of breaking free was not just a personal victory; it was a public testament to her strength and her willingness to confront painful truths.

Bethany's ability to open up about this chapter of her life has made her a powerful advocate for those who have similarly suffered in silence.

As a result of her revelations, Bethany's legacy has evolved from that of a successful actress to a figure of empowerment. Her openness has been a source of inspiration for many who feel trapped in their own circumstances. By sharing her story, she has shown that it is never too late to take control of one's life, no matter how insurmountable the obstacles may seem. This message is particularly poignant in today's cultural climate, where more and more public figures are finding the courage to speak out about abuse, manipulation, and mental health struggles. Bethany's contribution to this conversation is invaluable, and it cements her place not just as an entertainer but as a voice for healing and change.

In terms of her future projects, Bethany Joy Lenz continues to leverage her artistic talents while embracing new roles as an advocate and storyteller. She has co-hosted the *Drama Queens* podcast alongside former *One Tree Hill* co-stars Sophia Bush and Hilarie Burton Morgan, where they revisit the show and reflect on their personal growth since their time on set. The podcast has resonated with fans, not just for its nostalgic value but for the candid conversations the trio has about life, career, and womanhood. Bethany's contributions to these discussions, especially her insights into personal healing and resilience, further solidify her evolving legacy as someone willing to engage in difficult but necessary conversations.

In addition to her work in entertainment, Bethany has embraced writing, with *Dinner for Vampires* being one of the most anticipated projects of her career. The memoir is expected to provide even more detail about her decade-long involvement in the cult and how she managed to reclaim her life afterward. This book marks a significant turning point for Bethany, as it is not only an artistic endeavor but also a deeply personal one. Writing about trauma and recovery is no small feat, and Bethany's willingness to take on this challenge shows her determination to use her platform for something bigger than fame. Her book will likely stand as a key part of her legacy, offering readers insight into her inner world and, hopefully, encouraging others to seek healing in their own lives.

Looking ahead, it's clear that Bethany Joy Lenz is not finished making her mark on the world. While she may have started as an actress beloved for her work on a teen drama, her future is one that promises continued evolution. She has expressed interest in directing more projects, following her debut behind the camera during the final seasons of *One Tree Hill*. Her directorial ambitions align with her broader goal of telling stories that matter—stories that uplift, challenge, and inspire. Whether she continues in front of the camera, behind it, or as a writer, Bethany's legacy will be defined by her ability to push boundaries and reinvent herself time and time again.

Her personal life, too, plays a critical role in shaping her future. As a single mother, Bethany is deeply committed to providing a stable and loving environment for her daughter, whom she has credited as one of her greatest sources of strength. Balancing motherhood with her career and advocacy work is no small task, yet Bethany has shown that it is possible to pursue both professional fulfillment and personal joy. Her ability to prioritize her family while still pushing forward in her career adds another layer to her legacy—one of balance, love, and resilience.

Perhaps one of the most compelling aspects of Bethany's legacy is her refusal to let her past define her. While her experiences in the cult were undoubtedly painful and life-altering, she has chosen to use those experiences as fuel for her growth. Rather than shying away from the darkness in her past, Bethany has embraced it, understanding that it is a part of who she is, but not the entirety of her story. This level of self-awareness and courage is rare, and it is one of the reasons why she remains such a compelling figure in Hollywood today. Bethany's story is one of survival, but more importantly, it is a story of transformation. She is not simply surviving; she is thriving, and in doing so, she is providing hope to others who may feel stuck in their own struggles.